OUT AND ABOUT

Please return / renew by date shown.
You can renew at:
norlink.norfolk.gov.uk
or by telephone: 0844 800 8006
Please have your library card & PIN ready.

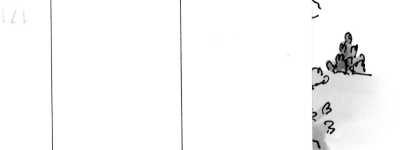

PLAYGROUP COLLECTION

17 JAN 2013

D1363109

Safety

NORFOLK LIBRARY
AND INFORMATION SERVICE

NORFOLK ITEM

30129 051 273 580

Llewellyn, Claire
Look out out and about
1.Accidents - prevention - Pictorial works - Juvenile
literature
I.Title II.Gordon, Mike III. Out and about
613.6

Printed in China

ISBN-13: 978 0 7502 5290 4

Hachette Children's Books
338 Euston Road,
London NW1 3BH

LOOK OUT!

OUT AND ABOUT

Written by Claire Llewellyn
Illustrated by Mike Gordon

WAYLAND

We spend a lot of time at home

and at school.

So in the afternoon or at weekends, it's great to get out and about.

Shall we go for a swim?

You go to many different places – the swimming pool...

the library...

the hairdresser.

In places like this there are lots of people, and lots of things to see.

7

Being out is not like being at home.

Everyone is busy
doing things.

Adults are not always
watching you as carefully.

So it's important to stick close to them.

Or what could happen?

Being lost can feel very scary.

You don't know any of the faces around you. You don't know what to do.

Whenever you are lost or feel a bit scared, it's important to ask for help. Who are the best people to ask?

A sales assistant

A checkout person

The information desk

These people will keep you safe until someone comes and finds you.

But what if you were lost
in a busy street?
What could you do then?

You could ask
someone for help.

A woman with a
child

A police officer

14

Or you could get help in a place you know.

The hairdresser

The library

Don't worry, you won't be lost for long.

15

It helps if you can tell people
the things they need to know.

Then they can call
someone to come
and find you.

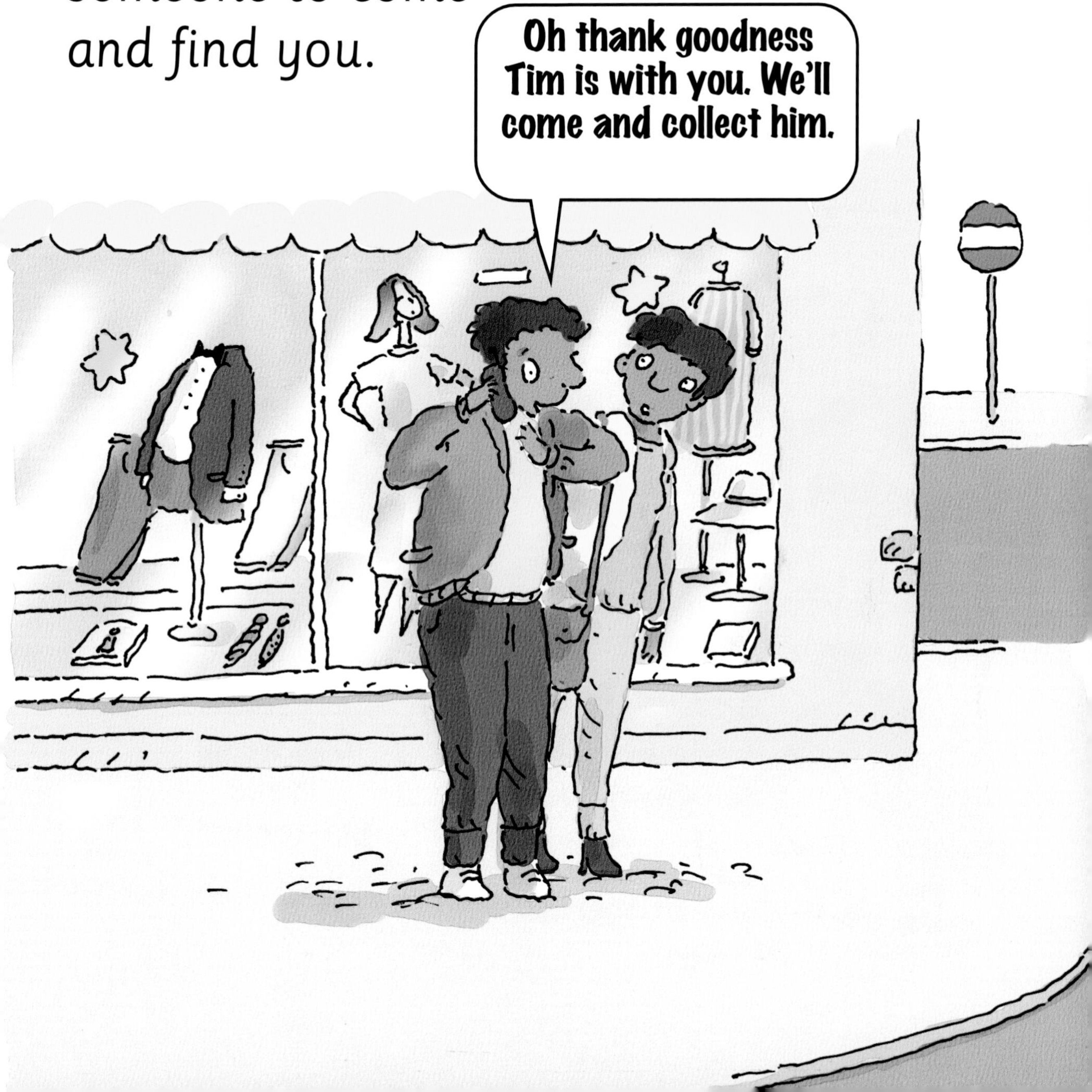

There are other ways of taking care of yourself when you're out and about. Think about when you go to the park.

Accidents can happen in playgrounds. How can you keep yourself safe?

Lots of people walk their dogs in the park. The dogs like to run around, sniffing.

Sometimes they want to sniff you.

You need to be very careful with dogs. Are they always friendly?

You meet all sorts of people when you're out and about. Most of them are very friendly.

But who is it that makes sure you are safe?

Mum

Dad

Gran

Grandad

Childminder

Make sure they always
know where you are.

Sometimes when you're playing outside, you feel like an explorer. You discover things you've never seen before.

Always try and play in safe places.
Keep away from railways and roads.
Keep away from water.

Play in open spaces
where people can see you,
or hear you if you call.

You can have lots of fun
when you're out and about.
Remember to take care
of yourself.

And, if things go wrong and you need a helping hand, always ask the right person for help.

Notes for parents and teachers

Look Out! Out and About and the National Curriculum

This book will help cover elements of the PSHE curriculum at KS1 (ages 5-7), in particular the requirement that children at this age "should be taught rules for, and ways of, keeping safe … and about people who can help them to stay safe". The Citizenship KS1 and KS2 schemes of work are also relevant. Activities relating to the scheme of work unit entitled 'People who help us – the local police' could include personal safety elements.

Issues raised in the book

Look Out! Out and About is intended to be an enjoyable book that discusses the importance of safety in public places outside the home or school. Throughout, children are given the opportunity to think about taking care of themselves and about what might happen if they do not pay attention to safety issues. It allows them time to explore these issues and discuss them with their family, class and school. It encourages them to think about safety first and the responsibility and practical steps they can take to keep themselves safe.

The book looks at the many places we go – to shops and parks, for example – and asks questions about what might happen in places like these when someone gets lost or separated from their parents or carers.

It is full of situations that children and adults will have encountered. It allows a child to ask and answer questions on a one-to-one basis with you. How can you avoid getting lost? Who would it be safe to ask for help if you were separated from your parents or carers? The amusing illustrations help to provide answers with ideas and suggestions.

Keeping safe in public places is important for everyone. Can your children think of an incident in which they lost sight of their parents or carers in a crowded place? How did this make them feel? Have they ever been tempted to play in places which perhaps were unsafe and where their carers could not see them? Are they confident about dealing with dogs? Are they aware of stranger danger? This book tackles all these issues. It uses open-ended questions to encourage children to think for themselves about the consequences of their behaviour.

Suggested follow-up activities

Make a list of all the different places you frequently go. What other people go to these places? Who could you ask for help if you were lost?

When might you need to phone the police and what number would you dial to do so? Think up a story in which you were lost. How would you feel?

Draw a children's playground, complete with swings and other equipment. Mark any potential dangers with a cross. How could you avoid accidents there?

Make a model of your street. Are there any safety hazards there? How could you keep yourself safe?

The Royal Society for the Prevention of Accidents (ROSPA) has a useful and informative website including fact sheets: www.rospa.com

Books to read

Dogger by Shirley Hughes (Red Fox, 1993)

Safety First: With Strangers (Franklin Watts, 2004)

Look Out for Strangers (Evans Brothers, 2003)